Uganda

Thailand

India

Thailand

China

Ukraine

Burkina Faso

Ecuador

Ecuador

"Jesus said, 'Let the little children come to me,
and do not hinder them, for the kingdom of heaven belongs
to such as these.' " *Matthew 19:14*

USA

Every Child Everywhere!

Written & Illustrated by

Debby Anderson

CROSSWAY BOOKS • WHEATON, IL

Iraq

A special thanks to:

Compassion International, especially Becky Tschamler and the Compassion photographers—Chuck Bigger (4-7, 11, 13, 15, 16, 19, 21, 22, 23, 25, 26, 35), Tom Kimmell (6), Keely Scott (30), and Philippe Mermod (35).

All those who helped to provide additional photos: Ben, Jenny, Joe, Kevin, and Gordon Anderson, Michael and Dana Ball, Pat Crumpton, Jennifer Kerr, Faith Okada, Noël Piper, Mackenzie Rollins, and my kindergarten students.

Korean calligrapher: Eun-Suk Unruh.

The countless friends, international students, missionaries, and neighbors who shared fascinating information about beautiful cultures from around the world.

Every Child Everywhere
Text and illustrations copyright © 2008 by Debby Anderson
Published by Crossway Books
      a publishing ministry of Good News Publishers
      1300 Crescent Street, Wheaton, Illinois 60187

Editor: LB Norton. Designer: Jessica Dennis.

Printed in Singapore.

Library of Congress Cataloging-in-Publication Data

Anderson, Debby.
 Every Child Everywhere / written and illustrated by Debby Anderson.
   p. cm.
 ISBN-13: 978-1-58134-862-0 (hc : alk. paper)
 ISBN-10: 1-58134-862-2
 1. Children (Christian theology)--Juvenile literature. 2. God-Love-Juvenile literature. I. Title.

BT705.A53 2007
242'.62-dc22   2007020191

I M G	17	16	15	14	13	12	11	10	09	08
14	13	12	11	10	9	8	7	6	5	4	3	2	1

For Katelynn and Jacey:
You are each God's beautiful artwork!
Love,
Nana

And for Yung Mee Park of Korea
Bulan Pupardthong of Thailand
Monica Aguero Rojas of Peru
Andile Holiday of South Africa
Mildred Aromo of Kenya
Arun VS of India—
Our sponsored children,
past, present, and future

Korea

안녕 하세요?

God loves every child everywhere! Near and far . . .

John 3:16

Brazil

Greenland

. . . in hot places and
cold places . . .

Ecuador

Austria

Ecuador

Ghana

India

Finland

Rwanda

El Salvador

Bolivia

Dominican Republic

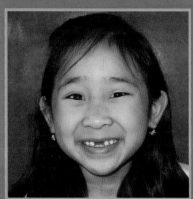

USA

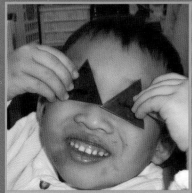

Vietnam

Haiti

Colombia

Ecuador

USA

Morocco

USA

Brazil

. . . He loves all of
our faces!

Matthew 18:10

His love for us is deeper
than the ocean . . .

Belize

. . . and higher than the sky.

Columbia

God would rather see
your smile than a sunset.

Psalm 36:5-7; Ephesians 3:17-19

Chile

Every child everywhere is made by God. You are God's artwork! From the top of your head to the tips of your toes, you are uniquely designed—one of a kind!

Genesis 1:26-31; Psalm 139:13-15;
Ephesians 2:10

Japan

New Zealand

Rwanda

Brazil

Sierra Leone

Chad

Nobody else thinks and feels just like you.

We are all different.

Some are faster . . . some are slower.

Some are smaller . . . some are taller.

Some are darker . . . some are lighter.

Some are louder . . . some are quieter.

And that's okay! That's what makes it fun to all be together!

Romans 12:4-6

Indonesia

We are different, but in many ways we are also the same!
Every child loves to play . . . inside . . . outside . . . upside down!

Mali

Portugal

Vietnam

Sweden

Israel

Netherlands   Pakistan

Children everywhere can help their families . . .

Ephesians 4:16

Guatemala

Canada

China

Papua New
Guinea

. . . and take care of their pets.

Wales

USA

Jordan

Ecuador

Peru

Djibouti

Zimbabwe

Children everywhere like to learn and explore!

Afghanistan

Guatemala

United Arab Emirates

"Hello . . . Mmolo . . . Litfukile . . . Re ya locha . . . Sanibona . . . Dumela . . . Goie more"

Jerome says "hello" in seven languages!

South Africa

Kazakhstan

Philippines

Poland

Ghana

Every child has hopes and dreams. Who you are now is the start of who you will become.

Jeremiah 29:11; Romans 8:37; Romans 15:13; Philippians 1:6

Israel

Mexico

Ben-Ami and Gustavo hope to be engineers.

Zepour hopes to be a doctor.

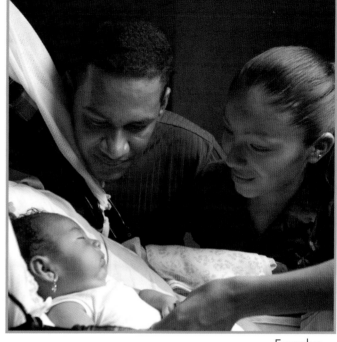

Ecuador

We all hope to have loving families.

Armenia

"With God all things are possible." *Matthew 19:26 ESV*

Every child everywhere is special to God! But being special doesn't mean we are perfect. We get into all sorts of troubles and problems and messes.

Even then God loves us and helps us to try again or to
try something new.

Deuteronomy 31:6; Philippians 4:13; 1 John 1:9

Ecuador

Guatemala

Tanzania

Always remember that God is everywhere and knows everything.
He is able to help every time. God sails on the wings of the wind,
but He is also right here with us.

Psalm 18:9-10; Psalm 139:7-10; Psalm 147:4-5

Japan

China

Malaysia

Winter   USA

Spring   Singapore

Summer   Jamaica

Fall   USA

Although God is busy keeping the seasons in place and
the planets spinning in space . . .

. . . He's never too busy to put a smile on your face! He holds
the whole universe together, but still He cares about you.

Genesis 8:22; Colossians 1:16-17; 1 Peter 5:7

God wants every child everywhere to joyfully celebrate life!

John 10:10; Philippians 4:4

England

Bolivia

USA

Nigeria

Argentina

Hong Kong

God loves every child everywhere forever and ever!
"He gathers the lambs in his arms and carries
them close to his heart."

Isaiah 40:11 NIV;
Psalm 127:3; Romans 8:38-39

*"Whoever welcomes one of these little children
in my name welcomes me."* Mark 9:37

Dear Friends and Family,

By reading this book you have already shown your love for children. The God-given potential in every child is a precious treasure. But globally, most children lack the resources to develop their potential.

Through Compassion's sponsorship program, you can help by sharing your own resources and God's love with a treasured child—a child whose name, photos, and letters will become treasures of your own.

But sponsorship is only one of many ways to help. All around us are children in our communities who need to know of God's love. Prayerfully consider the opportunities that God has given you to bring a smile to a child.

From the heart,

The Anderson Family

Asante! Thank you!
Kenya

Releasing children from poverty
Compassion®
in Jesus' name

1-800-336-7676 Compassion.com

A portion of this book's royalties will provide a sponsorship for another Compassion child.

"Whoever is kind to the needy honors God." Proverbs 14:31